TALES BY SAKI

Adapted For Stage

By
JULES TASCA

SAMUEL FRENCH, INC.
45 West 25th Street   NEW YORK 10010
7623 Sunset Boulevard HOLLYWOOD 90046
LONDON   TORONTO

Copyright ©, 1989, by Jules Tasca

ALL RIGHTS RESERVED

CAUTION: Professionals and amateurs are hereby warned that TALES BY SAKI is subject to a royalty. It is fully protected under the copyright laws of the United States of America, the British Commonwealth, including Canada, and all other countries of the Copyright Union. All rights, including professional, amateur, motion pictures, recitation, lecturing, public reading, radio broadcasting, television, and the rights of translation into foreign languages are strictly reserved. In its present form the play is dedicated to the reading public only.

The amateur live stage performance rights to TALES BY SAKI are controlled exclusively by Samuel French, Inc., and royalty arrangements and licenses must be secured well in advance of presentation. PLEASE NOTE that amateur royalty fees are set upon applica*tion in accordance with your producing circumstances. When applying for a royalty quotation and license please give us the number of performances intended, dates of production, your seating capacity and admission fee. Royalties are payable one week before the opening performance of the play to Samuel French, Inc., at 45 W. 25th St., New York, N.Y. 10010; or at 7623 Sunset Blvd., Hollywood, Ca. 90046, or to Samuel French (Canada), Ltd., 80 Richmond St. East, Toronto, Ontario, Canada M5C 1P1.*

Royalty of the required amount must be paid whether the play is presented for charity or gain and whether or not admission is charged.

Stock royalty quoted on application to Samuel French, Inc.

For all other rights than those stipulated above, apply to Samuel French, Inc.

Particular emphasis is laid on the question of amateur or professional readings, permission and terms for which must be secured in writing from Samuel French, Inc.

Copying from this book in whole or in part is strictly forbidden by law, and the right of performance is not transferable.

Whenever the play is produced the following notice must appear on all programs, printing and advertising for the play: "Produced by special arrangement with Samuel French, Inc."

Due authorship credit must be given on all programs, printing and advertising for the play.

Anyone presenting the play shall not commit or authorize any act or omission by which the copyright of the play or the right to copyright same may be impaired.

No changes shall be made in the play for the purpose of your production.

The publication of this play does not imply that it is necessarily available for performance by amateurs or professionals. Amateurs and professionals considering a production are strongly advised in their own interests to apply to Samuel French, Inc., for consent before starting rehearsals, advertising, or booking a theatre or hall.

No part of this book may be reproduced, stored in a retrieval system, or transmitted in any form, by any means, including mechanical, electronic, photocopying, recording, videotaping, or otherwise, without the prior written permission of the publisher.

ISBN 0 573 62560 3   Printed in U.S.A.

IMPORTANT BILLING AND CREDIT REQUIREMENTS

All producers of TALES BY SAKI *must* give credit to the Author of the Play/s in all programs distributed in connection with performances of the Play/s and in all instances in which the title of the Play/s appears for purposes of advertising, publicizing or otherwise exploiting the Play/s and/or a production. The name of the Author *must* also appear on a separate line, in which no other name appears, immediately following the title, and *must* appear in size of type not less than fifty percent the size of the title type.

FORWARD

Hector Hugh Munro (December 18, 1870 — November 14, 1916) is the British equivalent of O. Henry. Both were instinctive story tellers and loved practical jokes and surprise endings. Saki (Munro's pseudonym) filled his work with humor and irony; his claim to fame as a brilliant entertainer has been verified by critics as well as satisfied readers over the years.

One can gain insights into the comic artist by examining carefully the targets at which he or she chooses to point the devastating sword of humor. Saki often used his wit to skewer the complacent, the smug and the pretentious in English life at the turn of the century, in both Victorian and Edwardian periods.

Yet the tales stand the test of time and transcend the period in which they were written. Like all extraordinary comedy, these stories poke fun at those short-sighted actions and peccadillos of mankind that are universally the human experience. Who has never had a rival to release his jealousy as does Mrs. Packletide in *The Tiger*? Who has not known a friend or relative with the virtual pathological complacency of Johnathan in *The Unrest Cure*? And how many have had a house guest to get rid of in a hurry as the Songrails do in *The Hen*? How could one not laugh at the pseudo-art enthusiast that Saki limns in *The Background*?

Whenever Saki's ear or eye detected the overblown, the haughty, the rigid in his fellow Englishman, he went to work to make them laugh at themselves.

Munro took the pen name of Saki from *The Rubaiyat of Omar Khayyam,* in which Saki is the cup bearer who brings wine and joy to all. The English Saki, through his art, brought a heady intellectual pleasure and joy to us, his readers, by making us smile at a life that demands we do so often.

CONTENTS

THE TIGER............................. Page 7

THE UNREST CURE...................... Page 17

THE RETICENCE OF LADY ANNE......... Page 31

SECRET SIN .... Page 34

THE HEN .... Page 44

BLIND SPOT............................ Page 55

THE BACKGROUND .... Page 61

DUSK .... Page 69

THE TIGER

TIME: Early 20th Century England

PLACE: A drawing room

AT RISE: MRS. PACKLETIDE, a well dressed woman in her forties, is arranging tea and biscuits on a table. Satisfied that everything looks as it should, she crosses to a chair which is decorated with a tiger skin. She runs her hand across the pelt and laughs. There is a KNOCK at the door. MRS. PACKLETIDE crosses and opens it to LOUISA MEBBIN, a plainly dressed woman about MRS. PACKLETIDE'S age.

Mrs. Packletide. Louisa, do come in.
Louisa. Thank you, Mrs. Packletide. *(LOUISA Enters. MRS. PACKLETIDE closes the door.)*
Mrs. Packletide. It's such a pleasure to see you again.
Louisa. That's very nice of you to say so.
Mrs. Packletide. I've made some tea.
Louisa. I could use some, thank you. It's so cold. This weather has a way of reaching all the way inside a person.
Mrs. Packletide. That's the truth. I might not go out again until spring.
Louisa. Oh, I'd do that if I could too, Mrs.

Packletide. Hibernate.

Mrs. Packletide. *(pouring tea)* I think you just miss India.

Louisa. Yes, where we hunted was perpetual summer.

Mrs. Packletide. *(handing LOUISA a cup of tea)* It was an experience. You haven't seen the finished product, have you?

Louisa. *(crossing with her to the tiger pelt on the chair)* No. No, I haven't seen it all cured or whatever they do to tiger skins.

Mrs. Packletide. Run your hand over it. *(LOUISA runs her hand over the skin.)* So soft it almost makes you swoon, doesn't it?

Louisa. Rather.

Mrs. Packletide. My husband almost caught me on Saturday snuggling up to the darling prize.

Louisa. It would've been a treat to be here when you had the party and displayed this ... this prize to the press.

Mrs. Packletide. Really? Louisa, I never dreamed you'd be interested in being part of...

Louisa. You never inquired.

Mrs. Packletide. No, I ... it was so hectic that week that ... Do sit and enjoy your hot tea. *(They sit at the table.)*

Louisa. The only reason I bring it up is that ... well ... I thought since I was there with you in India, that I was the gunbearer and the lemonade carrier when you ... well ... killed the beast, that you would've perhaps had me around to ... I don't know ... corroborate how bravely you stalked the quarry, and how precise your aim was, and how calmly you...

MRS. PACKLETIDE. Louisa, whatever are you babbling on about? That affair I gave when we returned from India was a little gathering of close friends.

LOUISA. And I, Louisa Mebbin, am not to gather that close.

MRS. PACKLETIDE. Louisa?

LOUISA. Yes.

MRS. PACKLETIDE. I have the impression that you are perturbed about something.

LOUISA. Perturbed? Me? Just because I was left out of the biggest story to hit the society page since Loona Bimberton rode in in an aeroplane?

MRS. PACKLETIDE. But I said it was only the press and a small gathering of close friends. We were never close friend, you and I.

LOUISA. And Loona Bimberton is?

MRS. PACKLETIDE. What?

LOUISA. A close friend?

MRS. PACKLETIDE. You know how much I loathe Loona Bimberton.

LOUISA. She was here at the affair.

MRS. PACKLETIDE. She had to be here. You know that. Oh, Louisa, you know how I despise all my close friends and how they all can't stand me. You and I have never been close. In fact, I liked you from the first time we met and I hired you as a traveling companion.

LOUISA. So if we have a falling out, I can be counted in the next time you have a party?

MRS. PACKLETIDE. How silly. I must say you're acting rum today, Louisa. When you wrote and asked to stop by, I thought we would have a pleasant tea. Please tell me why you seem to have a quirk about something. *(MRS. PACKLETIDE looks at her watch.)*

LOUISA. Is there a hurry?

MRS. PACKLETIDE. Not an immediate hurry. But... well ... I can't sit — as we'd both love to — and let the afternoon go up in smoke. I do have my tiresome agenda to follow. *(LOUISA swallows her tea.)* Good Lord, I didn't mean for you to gulp, Louisa. No. It's just that besides my agenda, I have to keep a watchdog's eye on the kitchen or they'll over-salt the soup. The Bimbertons are dining with us tonight and they look for slip-ups of any kind.

LOUISA. I found out when you spared no time or expense to go tiger hunting in India how much you hate Loona Bimberton.

MRS. PACKLETIDE. That's why my husband and I try to see the Bimberton's as often as we can. You never know what your friends are up to behind your back. Best to keep an eye on Loona, especially now that I've made bigger headlines with that tiger than she made with a paltry aeroplane ride.

LOUISA. It's good that you told me that you're busy, or I might've dawdled and held you back. You see, my agenda for this afternoon is only this ... this pleasant tea.

MRS. PACKLETIDE. Ah, lucky Louisa. What a curse to have an agenda.

LOUISA. *(rising)* But knowing you have yours, I won't keep you. I wanted to see you today because...

MRS. PACKLETIDE. Yes ... Go on ... Is there something I

can help you with, dear Louisa?

LOUISA. Yes, dear Mrs. Packletide, there is.

MRS. PACKLETIDE. Have a biscuit and do tell.

LOUISA. *(taking a biscuit from the tray)* I will have a biscuit and I will do tell.

MRS. PACKLETIDE. Yes.

LOUISA. I've seen a week-end cottage near Dorking that I should like to buy.

MRS. PACKLETIDE. How wonderful. I think having a cottage in Dorking is so ... so ... so progressive. Getting out of the city and all that. Those cottages in Dorking, I must warn you, can be quite expensive.

LOUISA. Six hundred and eighty. The one I want.

MRS. PACKLETIDE. Six hundred and eighty? Quite a bargain, I'd say, for Dorking. Indeed a bargain.

LOUISA. I'm glad you don't think it's too much.

MRS. PACKLETIDE. *(rising)* For a cottage in Dorking, it's a steal.

LOUISA. I thought that too ... that it would be a steal. Only ... Only I don't happen to have the money to steal it.

MRS. PACKLETIDE. That's too bad.

LOUISA. Yes, but then I got to thinking how you could assist me.

MRS. PACKLETIDE. If there is anything my dear, dear...

LOUISA. I was your paid traveling companion to India. I am not a friend for you to loathe.

MRS. PACKLETIDE. And a very good traveling companion, I must say. And if there is any way, any reference, or any letter doused with praise that I could write on your behalf I wouldn't hesitate to...

LOUISA. Mrs. Packletide...

MRS. PACKLETIDE. Yes?

LOUISA. You can give me the money.

MRS. PACKLETIDE. The money?

LOUISA. You can give me the money for the cottage in Dorking. That's what you can do for me.

MRS. PACKLETIDE. What?

LOUISA. And a modest allowance for monthly incidental expenses.

MRS. PACKLETIDE. *(Laughs.)* Louisa, why in the name of the Lord of the blue would I want to take on the cost of your cottage in Dorking and incidental expenses?

LOUISA. Because you would not want your *close friends* or the press to know what really happened in India.

MRS. PACKLETIDE. Louisa?

LOUISA. How amused everyone of your friends would be if they knew how you got this tiger skin. *(She crosses to the chair on which the skin is draped.)*

MRS. PACKLETIDE. You ... You ... no one would believe you.

LOUISA. Loona Bimberton would.

MRS. PACKLETIDE. You wouldn't dare tell her about the...

LOUISA. I wouldn't have to tell her. The press would play this up big — the deception of it all. Loona Bimberton would read it. Oh, how it would gladden her heart to know that you became so jealous of the headlines she made by flying eleven miles in an aeroplane that you went to India to bag a tiger just to top her accomplishment.

Mrs. Packletide. Which I did. I got more photographs in the *Times* and more space and more...

Louisa. *(picking up the tiger skin)* But you told all the reporters this was a charging, rampant, killer tiger. *(She charges at MRS. PACKLETIDE with the tiger skin. MRS. PACKLETIDE gasps.)*

Mrs. Packletide. Louisa!

Louisa. More frightening and moving faster than when it was alive, I'll say, this aged, senile, toothless tiger that native children went up and petted.

Mrs. Packletide. The servants! Keep your voice down!

Louisa. My voice will be nothing to the loud laughter they'll hear when they find out how you tried to shoot this old grandpop of a cat as it slept ... under a tree.

Mrs. Packletide. Louisa, stop...

Louisa. Wearing a paper hat one of the children made for it.

Mrs. Packletide. I shall ring for Robert and have him show you the front door. *(She attempts to ring, but can't.)*

Louisa. Good. And I shall tell Robert how when you fired at this beast you missed and killed a blind man's goat.

Mrs. Packletide. You wouldn't give *that* away.

Louisa. That and more even. How hard would they all laugh, dear Mrs. Packletide, if they discovered that this tiger, with whom you made so many headlines, died of a heart attack at the sound of your gun when you killed the blind man's goat?

Mrs. Packletide. *You fiendish woman!*

Louisa. I am not. I just love that little cottage in Dorking so much that I ... I must have it.

Mrs. Packletide. You were such a nice paid companion, a joy to travel with...

Louisa. And I'll continue to be a joy, if you continue to pay.

Mrs. Packletide. Well, I refuse.

Louisa. *(replacing the tiger skin on the chair)* All right. You have a right to refuse. But I will stick to my word. I will got to the press.

Mrs. Packletide. You won't.

Louisa. I won't?

Mrs. Packletide. What you're doing here today is ... is criminal.

Louisa. Since when is reading a false story in the papers and then setting the record straight a crime?

Mrs. Packletide. You won't.

Louisa. To be true to my word now, I must, Mrs. Packletide. This time there'll be only one photograph of you. No gun. No pith helmet. No lemonade dripping from your brow as bogus perspiration. And under your picture will be the shameful story ... *(MRS. PACKLETIDE turns away.)* My flat is right by the newspaper office ... There'll be no inconvenience to me to just pop in and spill every little truth my insides hold ... *(MRS. PACKLETIDE makes no response.)* As you wish ... I suppose I should be going then if you have ... friends coming for dinner ... Odd, I thought you'd help me. Those weeks in India, I got to know you, got to know how much you really did hate Loona Bimberton ... I thought I could turn that much hate my way ... oh well, then ... goodbye. *(LOUISA starts for the door and begins to open it.)*

Mrs. Packletide. *(turning)* Come back here!

LOUISA. *(closing the door)* Mrs. Packletide?
MRS. PACKLETIDE. It will ... It will not ... not be necessary to go to the press.
LOUISA. *(pause)* Then...
MRS. PACKLETIDE. Yes.
LOUISA. Then what you're saying is...
MRS. PACKLETIDE. That's what I'm saying.
LOUISA. Oh, thank you. Thank you. I ... I ... I knew ... I knew you'd help me. I ... *(pause)*
MRS. PACKLETIDE. What ever the details are ... you know...
LOUISA. Oh, yes. I ... I will send the real estate broker around to see you tomorrow about the cottage and the expenses and...
MRS. PACKLETIDE. Yes ... Yes, do send him around.
LOUISA. I'm not a bad person, Mrs. Packletide. You know that. It's just that a woman like myself has few avenues for making her way to get where she wants to go.
MRS. PACKLETIDE. Just as few avenues as I have to go where I must go. So you see, I understand you, Louisa.
LOUISA. I thought ... to be honest ... I thought you'd be more hard-hearted after you agreed. You almost seem relaxed.
MRS. PACKLETIDE. But I am. I am relaxed ... dear Louisa.
LOUISA. So ... so it's settled then. I mean ... you've agreed...
MRS. PACKLETIDE. You're the one, Louisa, who needs to relax. It's settled. I said it was. And so it is.

LOUISA. It's a dream of a cottage. All white with red shutters and a red gate in the front yard and ... Excuse me for going on like this.

MRS. PACKLETIDE. It's understandable. It represents a new life in a way. I'll have to come and see it. I will come.

LOUISA. Oh, yes ... yes ... well ... then ... I know you're very busy now and ... well ... Good day. Good, good day to you, Mrs. Packletide ... and thank you. *(LOUISA again crosses to the door.)*

MRS. PACKLETIDE. Louisa. *(LOUSIA stops.)* Don't go. You must stay to supper, dear Louisa.

LOUISA. *(turning back)* You ... You want me to ... to...

MRS. PACKLETIDE. *(crossing to her)* Of course. You're here. You're dressed. I want you to meet Loona Bimberton.

LOUISA. Me to meet...?

MRS. PACKLETIDE. Yes, I've decided. I think she'll like you. I do think she will. And I think, yes, I think you'll like her. We ... We'll probably all become ... friends ... good friends. Oh, yes, I'm sure ... *(She takes LOUISA'S hands in her.)* Louisa, your hands are trembling ... dear Friend, what the matter?

(The LIGHTS fade on a wary LOUISA MEBBINS and her new "friend," MRS. PACKLETIDE.)

THE UNREST CURE

TIME: Early 20th Century England

PLACE: The living room of a country estate

AT RISE: MISS VICTORIA HUDDLE, a young woman, and CLOVIS, a young man dressed as a Protestant minister, pace. CLOVIS stops after a beat and pours a drink from a bottle of whiskey which is set on a table.

CLOVIS. It's a cruel trick to play.
VICTORIA. But necessary, Clovis. What else can we do?
CLOVIS. *(after drinking his whiskey)* You're asking me? I've never even met your brother. And now to meet and deceive him dressed like this.
VICTORIA. You do look like a real minister. I'll say that.
CLOVIS. Got to have the suit back to Reverend Kloster by 6.
VICTORIA. I appreciate your doing me this favor.
CLOVIS. And your family doctor thinks your brother Johnathan needs ... needs this?
VICTORIA. Yes. Dr. Bannister calls it the unrest cure.
CLOVIS. I dare say I've never heard that term before. The unrest cure.
VICTORIA. Dr. Bannister coined it himself. The unrest

cure. You've heard of a rest cure, Clovis.

CLOVIS. Of course, Victoria. Everyone's heard of a rest cure. A rest cure is for someone who's broken down under stress and strenuous living.

VICTORIA. Exactly. You see and Johnathan suffers from the opposite. Too much repose and placidity and dull routine.

CLOVIS. And J.P., your brother, is that stuck fast in repose and placidity and dull routine that you see the need to...

VICTORIA. Dr. Bannister said it's a true British illness. I myself see it as an indisposition that can afflict lesser peoples as well.

CLOVIS. Your brother is just too damned comfortable.

VICTORIA. Now you've pegged him. And Dr. Bannister says J.P. needs some great trouble to destroy the weave of trifles that has become his existence. Do you know if someone moves this whiskey bottle two inches, J.P. shakes all over at the change in it's position?

CLOVIS. One's liquor can become very important to one.

VICTORIA. Oh, J.P. doesn't even drink. He claims that liquor is for only weak-willed persons. This liquor bottle is still here only because when our father died, he left it here and here it must remain.

CLOVIS. I don't remember exactly where the bottle was.

VICTORIA. Doesn't matter. Today's the unrest cure.

CLOVIS. Yes. Yes, that is so. Is his heart good and strong for a rouse like this one that I've made up?

VICTORIA. Oh, yes. His heart is well protected from everything.

CLOVIS. Then he's fine.

VICTORIA. Well, he is in a bit of a snarl today because a thrush, that has built its nest year after year in the oak tree on the lawn, this year, for no obvious reason, is building in the ivy on the garden wall. J.P. told me at breakfast that the change is unnecessary and a mite irritating.

CLOVIS. My Lord, suppose it's a different thrush?

VICTORIA. Don't you think I suggested that? He said that would be more annoying. He said, "Victoria, I don't want a change of thrush at this time of life."

CLOVIS. This is a sickness. I can see it.

VICTORIA. He eats, sleeps, even scrubs his teeth — 12 times per tooth — according to the clock. If cook is even a hair's breath late with his mutton pie — Fridays at 7 — he stares out the window in deep distress at the disorder in the world.

CLOVIS. Well, I am here to be the kind of disorder. A puck to smash his clock and tear up his routine. *(He takes the mail from the table and tosses it underneath.)*

VICTORIA. That's his mail, Clovis.

CLOVIS. His mailman never got here today — part of the plot.

VICTORIA. Oh.

CLOVIS. I hope I can pull this off properly.

VICTORIA. You're one of the best actors in London. That's why I asked you to come up with something juicy.

CLOVIS. Yes, well, I think it is. Nothing I can put in a resume, though. The lead in J.P. Huddle's rest cure.

VICTORIA. Unrest cure.
CLOVIS. Unrest cure.
VICTORIA. And I thank you.
CLOVIS. You're thanking me, and I haven't done anything. Where is he?
VICTORIA. Patience, friend. He's reading *Country Life* in the morning room. When I told him a clergyman was here to see him, he simply said the intrusion was absolutely irregular.
CLOVIS. If he doesn't come soon, what I've planned is going to go amiss. I've sent telegrams out to Sir Leon Birberry and Mr. Paul Isaacs telling them to...

(JOHNATHAN HUDDLE, a staid, sedately dressed, middle-aged man Enters the room.)

VICTORIA. Johnathan.
JOHNATHAN. Yes. Look at this room. Look as if the devil himself swept through here. The label on this whiskey bottle always points to the southwest, Victoria. *(JOHNATHAN arranges the bottle to his satisfaction.)*
CLOVIS. I'm sorry. You see, I moved the bottle because I had...
VICTORIA. This is ... Reverend Clovis, Johnathan.
CLOVIS. Good day to you, Mr. Huddle.
JOHNATHAN. Yes, I'm sorry to have kept you waiting, but I hadn't planned to receive visitors today. My day's schedule doesn't leave a great deal of free time for ... for ... for whatever this meeting is about. I have the goldfish to feed at 11.
CLOVIS. I'm here about a matter of great importance.

You see, Mr. Huddle. I am the Bishop's secretary.

JOHNATHAN. *(impressed)* You are? You are the Bishop's — the Bishop's — secretary.

CLOVIS. His confidential secretary. He has others who only make tea.

VICTORIA. This is an honor, J.P.

JOHNATHAN. It is, but since father died, we have a small income, Reverend, that keeps us going, so we can't contribute more than we do now to the church or to the...

CLOVIS. Oh, I'm not here for money.

JOHNATHAN. Oh ... well ... then ... what ... what...

CLOVIS. Have you got a map of the area here?

VICTORIA. Yes, we do.

JOHNATHAN. *(stopping her from going to the desk)* I'll get it. You never fold it back the way it's supposed to be. *(JOHNATHAN takes the map out of the drawer and hands it to CLOVIS who opens it on the desk.)*

CLOVIS. *(examinng the map)* Hmmm. Hmm. Hmmm.

JOHNATHAN. What is it, my good man?

CLOVIS. The Bishop can hide out right ... here ... that is, until his car arrives.

JOHNATHAN. *(looking at the map)* Where? *(CLOVIS points to the map.)* Why must the Bishop hide out anywhere?

VICTORIA. *(trying to fold the map)* Yes, Reverend. And where is the Bishop now?

CLOVIS. Probably in town somewhere dressed as a barmaid.

JOHNATHAN. The Episcopal Bishop? Dressed as a barmaid?

CLOVIS. It's perfectly all right. His tips will all go to the missionaries.

JOHNATHAN. *(grabbing the map from VICTORIA and folding it correctly)* Will you get to the bottom of this, Reverend? I have a goldfish in there clamoring for food.

CLOVIS. Mr. Huddle, I must tell you since your home has been chosen by the Bishop himself.

JOHNATHAN. My home chosen for what?

CLOVIS. Miss Huddle, please, would you close the door and see that no servants lurk about? *(VICTORIA crosses to the door and closes it.)*

JOHNATHAN. Reverend Clovis, may I say...

CLOVIS. Shhhhh! Please be patient, Mr. Huddle.

VICTORIA. There's no one about, Reverend. They've gone to do the shopping. What is this business with the Bishop? It sounds so very ... so very stimulating.

JOHNATHAN. Victoria, do try to be more discreet in your conversation. Reverend Clovis, I'm going to feed my goldfish a quarter ounce of crushed insect bodies so if you'll be so kind...

CLOVIS. Your goldfish be dashed, sir! *Dashed,* do you hear?

JOHNATHAN. I ... I ... I'm ... I'm shocked. My pulse ... my pulse is ... is...

CLOVIS. Listen to me, Mr. Huddle. There's going to be bloodshed here today.

JOHNATHAN. Blood...

VICTORIA. Shed ... How baroque.

CLOVIS. The Bishop is out for blood.

JOHNATHAN. If he hadn't dressed up as a barmaid, this wouldn't have happened.

VICTORIA. What wouldn't have happened, J.P.?

JOHNATHAN. Whatever the Reverend is talking about happening.

CLOVIS. The Bishop is disguised as a barmaid only as a tactic. He's not sitting or laps and being pinched. He's planning.

JOHNATHAN. Planning what, Reverend Clovis? *(CLOVIS gathers them together.)*

CLOVIS. Today... today and on into tonight is going to be a great time, Mr. Huddle, in the history of Christianity.

VICTORIA. It is?

CLOVIS. Yes.

JOHNATHAN. Why?

CLOVIS. Listen to me. We are going to massacre every Jew in the neighborhood.

JOHNATHAN. Massacre the Jews?!

VICTORIA. Reverend Clovis. No. *(CLOVIS nods.)*

JOHNATHAN. What for? God, what for? Is there a general uprising against them?

CLOVIS. No, it's the Bishop's personal project. That's why he's here.

JOHNATHAN. But the Bishop is such a tolerant, humane man.

CLOVIS. That's why the surprise attack will be so effective.

JOHNATHAN. Reverend Clovis, go into town, to the bar. Tear the Bishop's dress off and speak to him.

CLOVIS. I couldn't do that. There are church laws, Mr. Huddle, against lifting a Bishop's dress.

JOHNATHAN. But, my man, the Bishop will be hanged.

CLOVIS. A car is waiting to carry him to the coast where a yacht waits. *(VICTORIA pours drinks for all from the whiskey bottle.)*

JOHNATHAN. There aren't thirty Jews in the whole neighborhood.

CLOVIS. We have twenty-six on our list. And they will all be dealt with.

VICTORIA. *(proffering the drinks)* Bracer, anyone?

JOHNATHAN. Victoria, it's eleven o'clock in the morning — good God, the goldfish.

VICTORIA. Oh, stop, J.P., you can give it extra bugs at the supper meal.

CLOVIS. We can all eat after it's done. *(VICTORIA drinks.)*

JOHNATHAN. This is a nightmare. Do you mean to tell me that you are planning violence against a man like Sir Leon Birberry? He's one of the most respected members of the community.

CLOVIS. He's down on our list. The Boy Scouts are to kill him.

JOHNATHAN. Boy Scouts?

CLOVIS. Yes, when they heard there was to be a real killing, they were keener than the men.

JOHNATHAN. This will be a blot on the twentieth century!

CLOVIS. And your house will be the blotting pad.

JOHNATHAN. Our...

CLOVIS. It's quite out of the way. Nothing much happens here. It's perfect.

JOHNATHAN. But I ... I ... I...

VICTORIA. Watch your pulse, J.P.

JOHNATHAN. How can you be so calm?

VICTORIA. I've taken a bracer.

JOHNATHAN. I thought we had a house rule about no

alcohol before 6.

VICTORIA. I needed something to still me.

JOHNATHAN. How could you be stilled by anything? We'll be included in this century's biggest scandal unless we do something.

CLOVIS. There's nothing to be done. Let's see, Mr. Paul Isaacs will be pushed down the staircase in there.

JOHNATHAN. But Paul Isaacs doesn't come here.

CLOVIS. He will be today. They all will be coming here. The Bishop sent them telegrams. Sir Leon will be run through in ... in ... Will the morning room be convenient?

JOHNATHAN. My sister and I shall go to the police!

CLOVIS. In the shrubbery are posted ten men, some of them deacons. They have orders from the Bishop to fire on anyone who dares leave this house without my signal of permission.

JOHNATHAN. Impossible! The post box is right up against the shrubbery. The postman would've seen them when he delivered my mail. Where's my mail? Victoria?

CLOVIS. The Boy Scouts — a few of the better knotters — strangled him an hour ago. *(JOHNATHAN staggers backward. He takes the whiskey and downs it.)*

VICTORIA. Careful, J.P., you spotted your tie.

JOHNATHAN. To hell with my tie, Victoria! Don't you see the tragedy about you?!

VICTORIA. Well, I'm trying, J.P., I'm trying. *(She takes another drink.)*

CLOVIS. There'll be nothing barbaric, I assure you. They'll all be killed cleanly and swiftly. The Bishop insisted on it. So you can see he is a gentleman as well as a Christian.

(We hear the sound of a car·HORN off. JOHNATHAN rushes to the window.)

   JOHNATHAN. It's Sir Leon!
   VICTORIA. Oh, no!

(We hear another HORN.)

   JOHNATHAN. And Mr. Isaacs!
   VICTORIA. God in heaven!
   CLOVIS. You'd better go to your room and read, Miss Huddle. We'll knock when it's all over.
   JOHNATHAN. Do as he says, Victoria!
   VICTORIA. *(Exiting)* Yes, J.P., as you say.
   CLOVIS. I'll be up stairs, Mr. Huddle, letting some of the deacons in through the window. Send Paul Isaacs right up. The Scouts will skewer Birberry in the morning room.
   JOHNATHAN. What makes you think I would take a hand in this?
   CLOVIS. You're a Christian. This is a High Church matter, Mr. Huddle. You have no choice. *(CLOVIS Exits. JOHNATHAN downs another drink.)*

(There is a KNOCK at the door. JOHNATHAN opens it to SIR LEON BIRBERRY and MR. PAUL ISAACS, two middle-aged gentlemen.)

ISAACS. Good day, Mr. Huddle.

JOHNATHAN. You both must get out of here!

SIR LEON. *(holding the telegram)* But we received these telegrams. "Urgent. Come immediately. Matter of life and death."

JOHNATHAN. Yes, your lives and deaths. Go. Go, I tell you.

ISAACS. What?

SIR LEON. Mr. Huddle.

JOHNATHAN. *(taking a pistol from his desk drawer)* Those telegrams were sent by the Episcopal Bishop.

ISAACS. The Bishop?

JOHNATHAN. In town dressed as a barmaid.

SIR LEON. You've been drinking, sir.

JOHNATHAN. No. I mean, only a bracer.

SIR LEON. *(to ISACCS:)* I can smell it.

ISAACS. You'd better stop pointing that gun, Mr. Huddle.

JOHNATHAN. Listen to me. They're going to massacre all the Jews.

ISAACS. Who is?

JOHNATHAN. *(pushing them out)* There's no time for explanations. I have it on the highest authority. Just do as I say. Go back to your automobiles and drive as fast as you can out of the district. I'll fire over the shrubbery to cover your escape.

SIR LEON. You're inebriated, Mr. Huddle.

JOHNATHAN. *(Exiting with them)* Go! Even the Boy Scouts are mixed up in it!

(CLOVIS and VICTORIA tip-toe on stage and look out the door.)

JOHNATHAN. *(off)* Quick, run for your lives, gentlemen!

(We hear SHOTS from JOHNATHAN'S gun.)

JOHNATHAN. Run!

(GUN SHOTS and the starting of AUTOMOBILES are heard.)

VICTORIA. I do think it worked, Clovis...

(We hear metal CRASH to the ground.)

VICTORIA. Oh my, he just shot the post box off. You'd better go now. The back way.
CLOVIS. I don't suppose after all this that your brother will be grateful ... for the unrest cure, I mean.

(The GUN FIRE continues as VICTORIA leads CLOVIS off.)

VICTORIA. Hardly. Since you've got him cursing, drinking and firing father's pistol wildly, it wouldn't be safe to tell him. Thank you again, dear friend. *(They kiss each other.)*

(JOHNATHAN re-enters just as VICTORIA pushes CLOVIS softly off.)

JOHNATHAN. *(holding up his smoking gun)* They got away,

Victoria! I've saved them! Where is he, that horrid cleric? Where?

VICTORIA. *(taking the gun)* When he saw you routed his band of followers and that the Jews escaped, he fled. He looked very frightened to me, J.P.

JOHNATHAN. And well he should be. *(He pours another drink.)* Bracer?

VICTORIA. Thank you, yes, please. *(JOHNATHAN pours her a drink. They both swallow the whiskey in one gulp.)*

JOHNATHAN. As soon as our pulses slow, we'll go down to the police station.

VICTORIA. Yes, J.P.

JOHNATHAN. Start a search party for the poor postman's body.

VICTORIA. Only Christian thing to do.

JOHNATHAN. Then I want to start a movement to disband the Boy Scouts.

VICTORIA. Yes, Johnathan. The blackguards.

JOHNATHAN. And I want to change churches.

VICTORIA. Since the Episcopal Church is finished now, we have no choice.

JOHNATHAN. Whiskey's almost gone. We should keep more in the house.

VICTORIA. We'll pick some up in town. Fetch the car keys. *(JOHNATHAN crosses to the door. Pauses.)*

(JOHNATHAN speaks as the LIGHTS slowly fade.)

JOHNATHAN. Security is an illusion, Victoria. When something as stable as the Episcopal Church can go mad that fast...

VICTORIA. Yes, there is hope for all of us.

JOHNATHAN. You've had too much to drink, Victoria. I fear this house will never be the same after today.

VICTORIA. *(as JOHNATHAN Exits)* And thank God for it.

(She hiccups, smiles and pours herself what is left of the whiskey into her glass as the stage goes DARK.)

THE RETICENCE
OF LADY ANNE

TIME: Early 20th Century England

PLACE: A drawing room

AT RISE: A woman lies on a sofa. After a beat, EGBERT, a foppish middle-aged man, Enters. He sees the woman.

EGBERT. Oh ... ah, here you are. I've been all over the grounds looking for you ... *(He pulls up a chair and sits. He cleans his glasses.)* Listen to me ... Dearest ... Dearest ... If I had known this sort of thing would have hurt you this much ... Anne, no personal harm to you was intended ... You see ... Dearest ... a man ... let me explain ... a man ... these women ... these other women, that is ... one ... one takes a certain interest in them, but only — how can I put this — only a sporting interest ... Oh, I know that sounds so cross and unfeeling, but there are certain pecadillos men have that ... Anne, it's like a good round of golf or something ... It's not as if one give's one's heart and soul over or anything ... *(Pause. EGBERT rises.)* I understand your feelings. I do. I understand your reticence to even address me. But Anne ... you ... you must admit that we ... we ... we do travel about a great deal ... one ... one meets people ... I'm sure you meet people also — not that

I believe that you would ever stoop to ... to ... that is to say ... you understand, when a man travels about, certain opportunities present themselves and — although he must use the utmost discretion in his selection — he ... what I'm trying to say Dearest Wife, is that these things happen and it in no way diminishes his admiration — deep admiration — for his wife ... Anne? Anne, this silent treatment that you so often resort to doesn't make this any easier on me, I might say. Oh, I know you do it to strike back, but you could have some consideration for my feelings. You know how I can't tolerate your closing yourself off like this. *(pause)* Anne? Anne, I'm sorry. In my clumsy way I've been trying to apologize. I'm sorry ... There, I've said it. Are you satisfied now? I'm only human. These ... these women seek me out and ... all right, I lost my senses at times. Mother always said I had no knack for disciplining myself ... It's ... I admit ... women ... that is ... Look, I have a little weakness there. All right, I admit it. But ... I'm not ... I'm not a bad husband when you get right down to it ... Oh, Anne, aren't we being silly? We're both adults who know how weak men and women can be and ... All right, Anne, suppose ... suppose ... suppose I promise — swear — not to stray from you ever again? Huh? Suppose I swear to it? Oh, I know what you're thinking: He's promised me before. After Laura and Amanda and — good God, Anne, don't have us start dredging them all up again. This time ... Anne, this time I am firm in my resolve to — how shall I put it — sin no more ... all right then? ... Anne ... I knew ... I knew when I walked into this room that this time ... Egbert, I said to myself, you've really done it ... *(Pause. He crosses down stage.)* So be it. You are right. I know this time it's different. I have crossed the line. God, I know what a heinous act I've committed. It was ... was particularly callous of me to ... Anne ... don't make me say it ... Why don't we change clothes and go for a ride? Morgan has polished the car ... Anne, we could be in London in two hours. We'll stay over ... Huh? ... Anne, this silence is agony! *(He turns to her.) At least curse at me! Rant at me! Say something! (pause)* As you wish. Then hear the truth about her. That fact that Lady Carlotta is your best friend does not mitigate the fact that she is a woman. And I might add a woman with as weak a will as I have when it comes to ... to ... She feels as disenchanted with herself as I do with myself ... Anne ... Anne, we spent only one night together ... Lucifer himself must have had us bump into each other in that hotel. We ... we had some drinks and ... well ... some damned foul adolescent passion ran out of us like an evil genie from a bottle ... Anne, we spent only one night together — one foolish night. In the morning we both realized that ... that what ... what we had done would ... would hurt you so ... and we ... we parted and vowed never to let it happen again. Anne ... Anne ... Damn that hotel maid for opeing her mouth to our cook when they ... Regardless of the outcome of this, Anne, I want that cook sacked! She had *no* business ... Well, I'll deal with her later. *(He sits and pulls his chair closer to her.)* Right now I want you to be the woman you've always been for me. *(He takes her hand.)* Strong. Understanding. I need that now. I need ... Anne. *(He turns her head. Her hand drops onto the floor.)* Anne! *(Her eyes and mouth are open. He jumps up.)* Good God, Anne, you're ... you're ... she's ... dead.)

(LIGHTS quickly fade.)

SECRET SIN

TIME: Early 20th Century England

PLACE: A parlor in a grand English home

AT RISE: A middle-aged woman, JANE TROYLE, Enters with a young man, HENRY TROYLE. JANE is angry and throws her shawl onto a chair.

HENRY. Aunt Jane, please calm down.

JANE. I can't. I simply can't. I expected that all the house guests we're having here for the week would be respectable.

HENRY. But you invited this Mr. Brope yourself.

JANE. Because I thought he was a dull enough person to keep grandfather company. A person should be what he seems, Henry. I will not tolerate anyone masking secrets. I like only real people.

HENRY. What secret is this Septimus Brope masking?

JANE. Would you imagine that Septimus Brope, the editor of *Cathedral Illustrated,* an expert on funerals and Byzantine worship would be...

HENRY. What?

JANE. Making love to my maid, Henry, that's what.

HENRY. Making love to ... well ... perhaps he got restless here all week. Grandfather cajoles him into reading to him every second he's awake.

JANE. If he craved excitement there was always a croquet game going on.

HENRY. I find it hard to think that a man who writes so delightfully about cathedral architecture and church crypts would choose a house maid. Are you sure?

JANE. He has the room next to mine and on more than one occasion I've heard him next door announcing "I love you, Florrie."

HENRY. And you think that your maid Florinda and Septimus Brope...

JANE. Addressing Florinda as Florrie certainly denotes that an unrespectful friendship has arisen.

HENRY. Well, you're not mincing words, Aunt Jane.

JANE. Fifty pounds to you, Henry, if you get him to break off the affair.

HENRY. *(very interested)* Fifty pounds? It means that much?

JANE. That's why I asked to have Mr. Lover Boy Brope sent up here to you.

HENRY. I see. But I can't fathom what I could do until there is some evidence that he really has...

JANE. Evidence? I heard him next door. I have the ears of a hawk.

HENRY. That's eyes, Aunt Jane, eyes of a hawk.

JANE. I have those too, nephew. As I was coming upstairs after breakfast Don Juan Brope was going to his room. This paper dropped out of a tablet he carried. *(She produces a sheet of paper.)*

HENRY. *(taking it and reading)* "I love you, Florrie. Meet me in the garden by the yew." Hmm.

JANE. His secret is out. And there's a yew tree at the

bottom of the garden near the tennis court. Beautiful spot. Your Uncle Charles often took me there — after we were engaged and always with grandfather as chaperone. There were no secret lives in those days.

HENRY. Maybe this Mr. Brope is behaving in an unseemly manner.

JANE. Another thing about this bizarre man.

HENRY. Is what?

JANE. His income. Grandfather says Mr. Brope only gets about 200 a year as editor of *Cathedral Illustrated,* yet he has a flat in Westminster and he goes abroad to the Greek Islands every year. He dress well and gives luncheons and ... well, you can't do all that on 200 a year.

HENRY. Suppose he writes for other magazines.

JANE. No, I inquired. He once tried the sports magazine with an article on churches in famous fox hunting centers, but it wasn't accepted.

HENRY. Then he must have other income.

JANE. Whatever else he does, he's not going to pass the time of day by using my maid's emotions as marionette strings to pull her this way and that.

HENRY. You certainly don't mince words, Aunt Jane. Can you be that concerned if Septimus Brope runs off with Florrie?

JANE. Florinda. A good maid is a treasure.

HENRY. Oh, come now, Aunt Jane. I can get you another maid in a flash, so I don't think you...

JANE. I don't want another maid. If you must know, it's my hair. I can't manage my hair. Florinda understands hair, how to curl it, comb it, color it. I would look like Medusa if I didn't have my Florinda.

HENRY. So that's your secret.

JANE. I have no secrets, Henry. I am as you see me. A well-off widow, unassuming, moral and upright enough to know when my maid and a house guest are committing...

(SEPTIMUS BROPE, a bespectacled, withdrawn, little man, Enters.)

HENRY. Ah, Septimus, come right in.

SEPTIMUS. Mrs. Troyle. Henry.

JANE. Good morning, Mr. Brope.

SEPTIMUS. Your grandfather told me someone wanted to see me up here and so...

HENRY. Yes, Mr. Brope. I think my nephew had something or other he wanted to ask you. You'll excuse me for a few minutes. I must go find out when Florinda can do my hair today. I'll be back. She's not just an ordinary maid, you know. She has a mind that was made to handle ... hair.

SEPTIMUS. Yes, Mrs. Troyle. *(JANE Exits.)*

HENRY. *(Crosses to SEPTIMUS.)* So, then, are you having a good holiday here?

SEPTIMUS. I consider it one of the best Easter weeks I've spent.

HENRY. Easter. Yes. Resurrection week. My aunt's happy that everyone she's invited is enjoying her hospitality. She asked me to see you today, actually.

SEPTIMUS. Oh?

HENRY. Yes, to inquire if everything is up to snuff. The

food. The staff.

SEPTIMUS. Oh, everything's fine. I couldn't ask for better food, better company...

HENRY. There's no need to dissemble with me, Septimus. I know what a bore Grandfather is. I'll come right to the point. I also know about ... Florrie.

SEPTIMUS. Oh ... Oh ... *(He sits.)* How ... How did you find out? *(HENRY shows SEPTIMUS the paper that his aunt gave to him.)* I ... I felt certain I'd dropped that somewhere. You won't give me away, will you? This sort of thing is nothing to be ashamed of but ... well ... it wouldn't do for the editor of *Cathedral Illustrated* to go in openly for this sort of thing.

HENRY. I should think not.

SEPTIMUS. You see I get quite a decent bit of money out of it.

HENRY. You mean you get money out of Florrie?

SEPTIMUS. Not out of her yet, but I will.

HENRY. I'm shocked. I think something should be said.

SEPTIMUS. Please don't. Oh, please.

HENRY. Tell me the truth. Have there been others ... others that you've extracted money from?

SEPTIMUS. Oh, yes. Yes, I confess it. But please don't breathe a word about this.

HENRY. I've never been in favor of one making a living by such means. How many others?

SEPTIMUS. Many others, Henry. For instance, "Cora with the lips of coral/you and I will never quarrel."

HENRY. How's that?

SEPTIMUS. That was one of my first hits. It still brings in

royalties. Then there's "Esmeralda, when I first beheld her" and "Teresa, how I love to please her." Both of those have been popular. Not all of them go over. Surely you remember "Lovely little Lucie/with her naughty nez retrousse."

HENRY. You're the song writer who wrote "Teresa how I love to please her?" *(SEPTIMUS nods. HENRY laughs.)*

SEPTIMUS. *(Rises.)* You shouldn't laugh. There's money in it, Henry. You understand the secrecy. Me, an authority on ecclessiastical architecture and liturgical subjects, writing "Cora with the lips of coral" and "Rhoda, Rhoda kept a pagoda."

HENRY. That was from your pen, too?

SEPTIMUS. Yes and "Maisy is a daisy," and "Dainty little girlie Mavis."

HENRY. I'm astounded. Truly.

SEPTIMUS. As I would expect. I can see the astoundedness all over your face.

HENRY. *(singing)* "Dainty little girlie Mavis?" *(SEPTIMUS nods.)* "She is such a rare avis?" *(SEPTIMUS nods.)* "All the money I can save is / all to be for Mavis mine."

SEPTIMUS. Don't sing any more. So you know. My sin is not a secret any more. Whom have you told?

HENRY. No one.

SEPTIMUS. You're the only one who know I script cheap music?

HENRY. As of now.

SEPTIMUS. Henry, it would be of some ... some value to you not to share this secret with anyone.

HENRY. Oh?

SEPTIMUS. Yes.

HENRY. How so, old friend?

HENRY. Well, I'm going off to the Greek islands next week. I could ... I could take you along — all expenses paid.

HENRY. The Greek islands. Hmm. That is something of value. And you have no interest in my Aunt Jane's maid, Florinda?

SEPTIMUS. Your Aunt Jane's maid?

HENRY. Yes, are you taken by her?

SEPTIMUS. Me? Henry, since you are — I trust — going to do me this favor and keep my secret, I'll tell you the truth: I'm something of, well ... a woman hater.

HENRY. You?

SEPTIMUS. Yes, I never could stand them.

HENRY. I know what you mean. I have similar sentiments.

SEPTIMUS. You do?

HENRY. We're the only two bachelors at the spring bash here.

SEPTIMUS. I've never thought of it that way. I just never thought that ... that...

HENRY. Fate. Fate is so arch.

SEPTIMUS. I agree and I've never heard it put so succinctly. Fate is so arch.

HENRY. This is a surprise ... Septimus. *(They shake hands.)*

SEPTIMUS. Henry. I am afraid that some of this woman hating has started to show up in my work.

HENRY. No.

SEPTIMUS. I've thrown out the lyric you hold in your

hand. The finished product reflects the senses of a man in need of holiday. *(He takes a sheet of paper from his pocket and hands it to HENRY.)*

HENRY. *(singing)*
HOW YOU BORE ME, FLORRIE
WITH THOSE EYES OF VACANT BLUE
YOU'LL BE VERY SORRY, FLORRIE
IF I MARRY YOU."

(They both laugh and JANE re-enters.)

JANE. I hope the frivolity is not at the expense of someone's good name.

HENRY. Oh, no, come in, Aunt Jane. It's just that Septimus and I have had a frank conversation.

JANE. Good.

SEPTIMUS. Yes. Your nephew, Mrs. Troyle, is a very easy-to-talk-to sort of fellow. I'm sorry we didn't get to know one another sooner. You'll have to excuse me now. Your grandfather waits for me. I'm reading my monograph to him on the Coptic church and it's relation to early Christian worship.

HENRY. Then have a good wild Coptic church read, Septimus.

SEPTIMUS. *(Exiting)* Yes. Thank you. And I look forward to seeing you both at lunch.

JANE. So?

HENRY. It's taken care of, Aunt Jane.

JANE. It is?

HENRY. Yes.

JANE. Splendid. What did he say? Did you have trouble?

HENRY. No. He admitted to the whole affair.

JANE. You see?

HENRY. Yes, he's quite serious about Florinda.

JANE. No.

HENRY. But I showed him how unsuitable and impractical the affair would be. The likes of him and a mere maid.

JANE. You're so dependable a young man, Henry.

HENRY. I also made a fervent plea for morality in a world that has left morality by the wayside.

JANE. You come from good blood, my dear.

HENRY. I told him a nice trip abroad would cool his dangerous infatuation for a servant. He agreed, but said he couldn't find someone to travel with on such short notice. He even asked me to go.

JANE. What did you say?

HENRY. Where would I get the money to travel abroad?

JANE. If you'll get that man out of here, *I'll* give you the money to go.

HENRY. Aunt Jane.

JANE. Along with the fifty pounds you've well earned.

HENRY. I don't know what to say. I couldn't take...

JANE. Why not. You're not doing it for yourself. You're doing a moral good, my boy.

HENRY. True, but...

JANE. Not another word. You wait right here and I'll draw up a check for you ... and Henry...

HENRY. Yes, Aunt Jane.

JANE. Not a word to your grandfather.

HENRY. Heaven forfend.

JANE. It'll be our little secret.

HENRY. *(as JANE runs off)* If you wish, Aunt Jane. *(He takes the sheet of music out of his pocket.)* Hmm. Septimus is right. So there is money in cheap music.

(He sings as the LIGHTS fade.)

HENRY.
"HOW YOU BORE ME FLORRIE
WITH THOSE EYES OF VACANT BLUE.
YOU'LL BE VERY SORRY, FLORRIE
IF I MARRY YOU
THOUGH I'M EASY GOING, FLORRIE
THIS I SWEAR IS TRUE
I'LL THROW YOU DOWN A QUARRY, FLORRIE
IF I MARRY YOU."

THE HEN

TIME: Early 20th Century England

PLACE: A British dining room

AT RISE: MR. ROBERT SONGRAIL and his wife, EDWINA, sit and have breakfast. ROBERT peruses a newspaper.

EDWINA. More eggs, dear?
ROBERT. No, thank you, Edwina. I've had enough. Your friend, Jane, never comes down to a good breakfast.
EDWINA. Jane always skimps on breakfast. Then she devours twice as much at lunch. Why does she worry so about her figure, I ask myself. I mean, she keeps a good distance from the opposite sex, so why does she bother to worry about...

(STURRIDGE, the butler, a rigid-looking, older man, Enters.)

STURRIDGE. Sir, madam, excuse me. But a messenger has just come from Mrs. Dora Bittholtz.
EDWINA. Oh?
STURRIDGE. Yes, madam, young chap on a bicycle. He said to inform you both that Miss Bittholtz shall be coming this Thursday.
ROBERT. Thank you, Sturridge. *(STURRIDGE Exits.)*

EDWINA. *(Rises.)* Dora Bittholtz on Thursday. God, Robert, she's coming a week early.

ROBERT. Dora always was a trifle unpredictable.

EDWINA. But now what do I do?

ROBERT. Have Sturridge get the maid to make a room up for Dora. That's simple enough.

EDWINA. You don't understand. Jane up there is staying with us for two weeks.

ROBERT. Edwina, there's plenty of room for both Jane and Dora.

EDWINA. Robert, Jane and Dora hate each other.

ROBERT. They do? *(She nods.)* How very awkward.

EDWINA. Hate so thick you'd think they were blood relatives.

ROBERT. *(rising)* How did this happen?

EDWINA. It was over a hen.

ROBERT. A hen?

EDWINA. It was a prize winning hen. Dora sold it to Jane for a fortune. Jane thought she'd breed this prize winning hen and get her money back by selling the pedigree chickens.

ROBERT. Good business sense.

EDWINA. But it turned out the hen wouldn't lay — ever. Not one blessed egg.

ROBERT. The hen wouldn't lay?

EDWINA. No.

ROBERT. Well, the animal world is different from us, Edwina. They lack a sense of duty.

EDWINA. Be that as it may, Jane wanted her money back from Dora. Dora refused. They fought. Teeth bared and claws waving, they fought.

ROBERT. Oh, my.

EDWINA. The abusive language they fired toward one another could've run electric lights, Robert.

ROBERT. Couldn't some friend — you, for instance — help them make up?

EDWINA. I tried, Robert. I tried. In person and by mail. I tried to engender an end to their quarrel.

ROBERT. And?

EDWINA. And I made it worse, I think. Just when I thought they were both softening their hard hearts, Jane cut the head from the reluctant hen and sent it to Doris by messenger with a note which read, "If only I could do to you what I have done with your sterile bird."

ROBERT. What? That is rather thick. You're right. It won't do to have them together warring under our roof. I'm a light sleeper as it is.

EDWINA. So what are we to do? Jane Martlet won't leave until her two weeks are up. I know her. And when she sees Doris, why, she'll just relish another battle.

ROBERT. This is a proper British home. I will not have raised voices here.

EDWINA. How will anyone evict Jane from her stay here early without a brass band of protest?

ROBERT. I suppose by in some way making Jane want to leave of her own accord.

EDWINA. There's not much chance of that. She loves it here. *(ROBERT crosses to the mantle where a large sword hangs and picks up his pipe which he proceeds to light.)*

ROBERT. Yes, she does love it here. In some way we must change that.

EDWINA. You wouldn't be rude to her.

ROBERT. I'm never rude to anyone. If I get her out of this house, it will be in a totally civilized manner.

EDWINA. It would be a miracle if you could.

ROBERT. *(fingering the sword)* I think I can.

EDWINA. You can?

ROBERT. Hens I know nothing about, but house guests...

(We hear a woman HUMMING.)

EDWINA. Shhhh. Here she comes. I'm leaving whatever mischief your mind's dredged up to you. I'll be picking roses in the garden.

(EDWINA Exits. ROBERT sits back down and pours himself more morning tea. After a beat, JANE MARTLET Enters cheerfully.)

JANE. Good morning, Robert.

ROBERT. Oh, Jane, please, sit down and have tea and toast.

JANE. No toast. I will have some tea, thank you. *(She sits and pours herself tea.)* Where's Edwina?

ROBERT. Oh, fooling in the garden as usual.

JANE. And you? How are you this morning? You look troubled.

ROBERT. *(rising)* Can't hide anything from you, can I, old friend?

JANE. I do have a sixth sense about trouble. Is it something I can help you with, Robert?

ROBERT. You're very kind. But no. I'm afraid this is a

household problem.

JANE. Oh?

ROBERT. Servants.

JANE. Servants?

ROBERT. They can be such a nuisance.

JANE. I thought you and Edwina have been wonderfully lucky in your servants. Sturridge, for one, is the model butler, and he's been with you for years.

ROBERT. That's the problem. When they've been with you for years, they become like part of the family. And you know how unpleasant family can become. Sturridge is the problem of which I speak.

JANE. I can't believe it. Sturridge is excellent.

ROBERT. I know he's excellent. We couldn't get on without him.

JANE. Then I don't understand.

ROBERT. Time. Time has taken it's toll. All this orderliness. Have you ever considered what it must be like to go on days without end doing the correct thing at precisely the correct time?

JANE. No, I've always had others who did that for me.

ROBERT. Such as a butler. Exactly. From polishing the silver to putting out the cat. To be noiseless, yet omnipresent. To be thorough, yet unobtrusive. To be all knowing to the other servants in matters of manners, morals and protocol of every stripe, and yet remain humane and personable.

JANE. Oh, I can only be personable for an hour a day. Longer than that, Robert, I'd go mad. I would.

ROBERT. That's it. You do understand.

JANE. Understand what?

ROBERT. Sturridge. Sturridge has gone mad.

JANE. No. It can't be. I just saw him polishing the brass on the front door.

ROBERT. Was he mumbling to himself again?

JANE. No. No. Mumbling to himself? He ... he talks to himself? I mean, all he did was nod and smile at me.

ROBERT. A smile is often madness breaking through like sunlight penetrating a ... a cracked wall.

JANE. He did smile. I can attest to that. He did smile. He did.

ROBERT. He's all right most of the time. He nodded and smiled?

JANE. Yes. Nodded first. Then smiled. The poor man.

ROBERT. It is a shame. At times, he's subject to delusions — obstinate delusions.

JANE. What sort of delusions?

ROBERT. Unfortunately ... Unfortunately they ... they...

JANE. *(rising)* Robert, what is it?

ROBERT. You see, Jane, these delusions usually center around ... around guests who stay with us.

JANE. Oh?

ROBERT. Yes. I remember when he took it into his head that Matilda Sheringham was the prophet, Elijah.

JANE. Matilda Sheringham? The prophet Elijah?

ROBERT. Yes. He remembered from his Bible that ravens fed Elijah in the desert, so he refused to seat her at meals and skipped her whenever he brought in the food, believing that Matilda was being fed by a catering service of black birds.

JANE. I've heard that insanity can be very abnormal.

ROBERT. You do have keen insights, Jane. I've always said that about you. Abnormal, however, is being charitable.

JANE. Sturridge is worse than abnormal?

ROBERT. To be sure. We had to sneak food to Matilda and in the end she cut her visit short and left.

JANE. I would've humored the man. I wouldn't've run off.

ROBERT. It's not always wise to humor the insane.

JANE. Good Lord, Robert, are you saying Sturridge might be dangerous?

ROBERT. One could never be certain. He's got a new wrinkle now.

JANE. Which is?

ROBERT. Oh, my, how do I begin? *(Pause. ROBERT crosses away from her.)*

JANE. It's quite all right. You can be honest with me.

ROBERT. Jane. Dear, dear woman...

JANE. It's me he's focused on now, I'll wager.

ROBERT. As a matter of fact...

JANE. Who on earth does Sturridge think I am?

ROBERT. Well, Jane...

JANE. Out with it, Robert. I must know the worst.

ROBERT. Jane. Dear Jane. He, Sturridge, thinks that you are ... Queen Anne. Anne Boleyn.

JANE. Henry the Eighth's wife?

ROBERT. Yes.

JANE. Who was beheaded?

ROBERT. The same.

JANE. And what has this crazed servant said about me?

ROBERT. Queen Anne's dead. That's what he said.

JANE. Of course Queen Anne's dead. And does he take me for the ghost of Queen Anne?

ROBERT. Oh, my no. He would never have smiled and nodded at you just now if he thought you were a ghost. I hope all this isn't frightening you.

JANE. Of course not. *(She crosses to the door and looks out. Then she crosses back to ROBERT.)*

ROBERT. What's he up to now?

JANE. Still polishing the brass. He nodded and smiled at me again.

ROBERT. You see? There's no hope.

JANE. No?

ROBERT. It's the very fact that you're alive that perplexes him. Something is wrong to him because you — that is, Queen Anne — live and breathe.

JANE. And I'm not going to change life-long habits for a servant. Did you explain to him that I am Jane Martlet, and not Queen Anne?

ROBERT. Edwina and I both did. He just smiled and said we couldn't fool him.

JANE. Sturridge wouldn't become ... hostile?

ROBERT. I didn't become alarmed until this morning.

JANE. What happened? What did he say?

ROBERT. He kept muttering to Edwina and me: "Ought to be dead. Long ago. Someone has to do it," he said.

JANE. This is awful.

ROBERT. That's why I mention the matter to you. Edwina's upset too. She's out there in the garden wondering what to do.

JANE. Are you saying Sturridge might kill me at any moment?

ROBERT. Not at any moment. He's busy with the brass work now.

JANE. I think you should reprimand him immediately, Robert. Give him a choice between this annoying insanity and unemployment. If he refuses to regain his sanity, I would discharge him.

ROBERT. I don't know. Good help is hard to find. But I'll try it if you think it'll work.

JANE. I don't want to be around when you tell him. He might go off at me or something. I have a few letters to write in the morning room, and then I shall go out and join Edwina in the garden.

ROBERT. All right, Jane. I'll take your advice. You seem to have such keen insights about people. *(JANE Exits and ROBERT rings for STURRIDGE. Then ROBERT crosses to the sword on the mantle and begins to finger it.)*

(STURRIDGE Enters.)

STURRIDGE. Sir?

ROBERT. Ah, Sturridge, yes. I wish you could do a favor for Miss Martlet.

STURRIDGE. Very good, sir.

ROBERT. She's in the morning room writing letters. She wants to copy the latin inscription from this old sword. I want you to take it to her.

STURRIDGE. Yes, sir. *(He crosses to the sword.)*

ROBERT. And Sturridge.

STURRIDGE. Yes, sir.

ROBERT. Take it without the sheath. It'll be less trouble.

STURRIDGE. As you wish, sir. *(STURRIDGE draws the blade and Exits.)*

(We hear JANE scream. ROBERT lights his pipe. STURRIDGE re-enters with the sword.)

STURRIDGE. For some reason, Sir, Miss Martlet seemed disinclined to copy the inscription just this moment. She just bolted from the morning room.

ROBERT. Then perhaps some other time. you know how moody women are.

STURRIDGE. I do, sir.

(EDWINA Enters.)

EDWINA. Good Lord, Robert! What's been going on? Jane refuses to come back into the house. And she wants you to drive her to the train station immediately. How ever did you do it?

ROBERT. It's her decision, dear.

EDWINA. However you managed this, I thank you. I'm to go up and pack her things. *(EDWINA Exits.)* Sturridge, do put that sword away. You look like the angel of death or something.

STURRIDGE. Yes, madam. Begging your pardon, sir,

but do I take it that Miss Martlet is cutting short her stay here?

ROBERT. Yes, Sturridge, that's quite correct.

STURRIDGE. *(replacing the sword in its sheath)* Oh, I am sorry, sir. Miss Martlet is such a nice guest.

ROBERT. Yes, but don't lose the moral of the whole story.

STURRIDGE. *(as the LIGHTS slowly fade)* The moral, sir? Which moral is that?

ROBERT. *(Exiting)* Beware of a hen who doesn't lay, Sturridge.

STURRIDGE. Yes, sir. Very good, sir ... 'Tis a sentiment to live by, sir...

(STURRIDGE, puzzled, tries to figure it all out as the stage goes DARK.)

STURRIDGE. I think...

BLIND SPOT

TIME: Early 20th Century England

PLACE: A British dining room

AT RISE: An older portly gentleman, SIR LULWORTH and a younger man, EGBERT, Enter. They both wear black arm bands. They cross to the table set for lunch. SIR LULWORTH pours them both drinks. Then he sniffs.

LULWORTH. Ah, my nostrils are trembling. No one cooks a goose like Sebastian.

EGBERT. Uncle, there is some business I must discuss with you.

LULWORTH. Discuss business? Now? Would that be respectful? We've just buried great Aunt Adelaide? Besides, we haven't even eaten, my boy. Sebastian cooks goose in some kind of Rhenish wine. You can smell the...

EGBERT. Uncle, listen to me. I've been going over Aunt Adelaide's papers and there's unsettled business to go over.

LULWORTH. Unsettled? You're Aunt Adelaide's principal heir. This house, the grounds. It's all yours. And I'm sure Sebastian will stay. Have you tasted a Sebastian salad? God, he makes it with olives. You don't have to force anything. You just naturally over-eat everything.

EGBERT. Could you stop talking about food for a moment and listen? Aunt Adelaide had all her letters and...

LULWORTH. There must be reams of family letters.

EGBERT. There are. More from her brother, Peter, than from anybody.

LULWORTH. He wrote to her daily. Poor Peter. What a tragedy.

EGBERT. A tragedy that's never been explained.

LULWORTH. What?

EGBERT. What happen to Uncle Peter has never been fathomed.

LULWORTH. Of course it has. He slipped on a garden staircase, Egbert. He slipped and fractured his skull in falling.

EGBERT. The medical evidence proved he was struck from behind.

LULWORTH. I heard that fairy tale. But they had medical experts testify that — you can smell the pudding, can't you, Egbert? Sebastian makes it with brandy. God bless talent. If I thought I could keep it out of the newspapers, I'd kiss Sebastian. The Michel-angelo of culinary art.

EGBERT. But was it such a fairy tale?

LULWORTH. Was what such a fairy tale? Haven't you got the decency to smell Sebastian's work? Inhale, my boy, inhale, for tomorrow ye may die, eh?

EGBERT. Was it such a fairy tale that Uncle Peter was struck a fatal blow on the head from behind?

LULWORTH. Who'd have a motive to destroy a canon of the established Church?

EGBERT. His cook who then became Aunt Adelaide's

cook was suspected.

LULWORTH. Only, my boy, because Sebastian was the only person around when the accident occurred.

EGBERT. But...

LULWORTH. But nothing, Egbert. Nothing could be sillier. Sebastian had nothing to gain by popping Peter on his pate. The canon paid him a pretty wage. And Sebastian kept Uncle Peter's digestion on perpetual holiday.

EGBERT. Uncle...

LULWORTH. *(Sniffs.)* He bakes his own biscuits, you know. If you sniff between the goose and the pudding, you can smell the devils getting ready to take your will power to hell. *(He sniffs again.)*

EGBERT. Sebastian is hot tempered, Uncle.

LULWORTH. This is Aunt Adelaide's funeral lunch, Egbert. Please don't make it a sad occasion. Sebastian has a hot temper because he's Southern French. I even think his mother was Italian. He must wax hot once in a while. It's a matter of bloodline overcoming propriety, my boy.

EGBERT. He nearly killed the gardner's boy once here for bringing him parsley instead of oregano.

LULWORTH. Nearly and altogether are world's apart. It's an egg dish he makes with oregano. I've had it here before. Ground cheese and beaten eggs and oregano. You can't use parsley. It would be a crime against Sebastian's art. The gardner's boy should have been ... well ... at least ... slapped around hard.

EGBERT. Why are you dismissing out of hand the possibility that Sebastian did have some lapse and...

LULWORTH. Because there had never been any quarrel

or argument between Uncle Peter and his cook. They proved that at the inquest. That's why Aunt Adelaide took Sebastian in here afterwards. I think she wanted to make up for the fact that the poor man was even suspected.

EGBERT. Ah, this is precisely the serious business I have to discuss with you.

LULWORTH. What is it then?

(SEBASTIAN, a cook, opens the door and sticks in his head.)

SEBASTIAN. In a few moments, you eat, Sir Lulworth.

LULWORTH. Yes, Sebastian, we can smell the meal nearing the finsih line, old man. God bless you. *(SEBASTIAN returns to the kitchen.)* What charge would you make against a saint on loan to us from the kitchen of heaven, I'm sure? His borsch should be in a museum. His souffles break down men's reason. His lemon cream tarts are ... *(EGBERT takes out a letter and holds it up to SIR LULWORTH.)* Now what is that?

EGBERT. One of the canon's numerous letters to Aunt Adelaide. Written a few days prior to his "accident." She must've only half read it, or she'd've spoken up at the inquest.

LULWORTH. Uncle Peter wrote more letters than Saint Paul wrote to the Ephesians.

EGBERT. Aunt Adelaide — rest her soul — should've read all of this one. I'm skipping down now. *(He reads.)* "I very much fear I shall have to get rid of Sebastian. He cooks divinely, but he has the temper of a fiend or an anthropoid ape, and I really fear him. We had a dispute as to the correct lunch to be served on Ash Wednesday, and I got so irritated and annoyed at his arrogance that I threw coffee in his face and called him a know-it-all Catholic..."

LULWORTH. The fool. Sebastian's genius transcends religious parochialism!

EGBERT. *(Continues reading.)* "I laughed at his threat to kill me. I thought the argument would blow over. But I sense that he is dogging my footsteps at night when I walk in the garden." *That's* where Uncle was found dead on the garden steps.

LULWORTH. *(taking the letter)* Sebastian?

EGBERT. Yes, Sebastian?

LULWORTH. *(examining the letter)* Hm. Hm. Hm. Have you shown this to anyone else?

EGBERT. No, but if lack of motive saved Sebastian from prosecution, this letter in the hands of the police will change all that. You can take it down to them yourself if you ... *(LULWORTH lights a match and puts it to the letter.)* Uncle! No! *(He tries to stop his uncle, but the letter is a blaze in his uncle's hand)*

EGBERT. *What in heaven's ... What have you done?! That was the evidence!*

LULWORTH. That's why I destroyed it. That's why Aunt Adelaide never came forth with it at the inquest. Of course, she read the letter. She read all Uncle Peter's letters.

EGBERT. But why should she wish to conceal her brother's murderer?! And why would you? A common murderer?

LULWORTH. A common murderer, possibly. But as Aunt Adelaide and I know, a very uncommon cook.

EGBERT. You can't possibly excuse...

LULWORTH. Fret not another moment. As soon as lunch is over, your problem with Sebastian will be over.

EGBERT. It will?

LULWORTH. Yes. I shall hire him for my own home.

(SEBASTIAN Enters carrying a large covered pan which he sets down on the table.)

SEBASTIAN. *(as the LIGHTS fade)* Voila! Lunch is served! Your goose is cooked! *(SIR LULWORTH smiles boradly at EGBERT as SEBASTIAN lifts the lid on his masterpiece.)*

THE BACKGROUND

TIME: Early 20th Century Italy

PLACE: An Italian court room

AT RISE: A POLICE OFFICER stands at the door. ARCHIE DELANCY, a man in his thirties, sits with his head in his hands. After a beat, a middle-aged JUDGE Enters absorbed in a folder of papers and photographs. He stops and looks at DELANCY.

JUDGE. A sad state of affairs. A very sad state of affairs.

ARCHIE. Your Honor? Are you the judge? Are you the authority here?

JUDGE. Of course. I'm not sitting up here to catch the breeze.

ARCHIE. Thank God! I've not been allowed to see a lawyer.

JUDGE. You will only need a lawyer, Signor ... Delancy?

ARCHIE. Archie Delancy. That's correct, Your Honor.

JUDGE. You will only need a lawyer, Signor Delancy, if there is to be a trial. This is an inquiry only.

ARCHIE. Thank God.

JUDGE. I wouldn't thank God so fast, signor. I've seen men broken before at these preliminary hearings.

ARCHIE. But I haven't done anything wrong.

JUDGE. Everyone has done something wrong. It's just a matter of time before one is caught, no?

ARCHIE. No. I'm not a criminal.

JUDGE. Don't sell yourself short, signor.

ARCHIE. This is unfair.

JUDGE. Italian courts make no claim to fairness, only to justice. *(To the Policeman at the door:)* Bring in the Signora Pincini. *(The POLICE OFFICER Exits.)*

ARCHIE. *(rising)* But she doesn't know the whole story.

JUDGE. Be at rest. We'll piece it together so it points the finger at someone.

ARCHIE. But there's no need to...

JUDGE. Signor, this has become a national matter in Italy.

ARCHIE. But, Your Honor, I am a British subject.

JUDGE. The court shall overlook your past indiscretion.

ARCHIE. I want a lawyer.

JUDGE. I said we're only inquiring. There's no need ... yet.

(The POLICE OFFICER Enters with an Italian WOMAN in black who is crying.)

POLICEMAN. Your Honor, Signora Pincini, widow of the great Andreas Pincini. *(The POLICEMAN goes back to the door.)*

ARCHIE. Signora Pincini, you have my deepest sympathy. Andreas was a brilliant artist. *(She spits in his face.)* Signora!

JUDGE. Signora Pincini, you will kindly address your remarks to the bench. First, is this the man your husband, Andreas Pincini used as a background?

SIGNORA. Yes, yes, Your Honor.

JUDGE. This man, Archie Delancy of Great Britain, sought out your late husband, Andreas Pincini?

SIGNORA. Yes, it was him.

JUDGE. For what purpose did he seek him out?

SIGNORA. He came to our village looking for my husband, one of the most famous artists in all of Europe to commission a work, Your Honor.

ARCHIE. I'm an art connoisseur, Your Honor, not a criminal. *(SIGNORA PINCINI spits in ARCHIE'S face again.)*

JUDGE. You're upsetting a woman in mouring, signor.

ARCHIE. She spat on me twice. Can't you hold her in contempt?

JUDGE. And why should I? She didn't spit on me. Signora Pincini, painful as it may be, tell me what happened.

SIGNORA. He — this devil — came to our village and asked that great artist, my husband Andreas... to... to do a work for him. He said he was interested in *the fall of Icarus.*

JUDGE. The one who flew too close to the sun, and the wax that held his feathers melted, and he fell to his death — that Icarus?

SIGNORA. Yes, Your Honor, he wanted Andreas to do it, the fall of Icarus.

JUDGE. So? Go on.

SIGNORA. Only he wanted the drawing tattooed ... tattooed on his back.

JUDGE. The fall of Icarus on his back. The photographs I have here of Signor Archie Delancy's back ... *(He shows her the pictures.)* ... Is this your husband's work?

SIGNORA. It's beautiful. Yes, it's his. Everything Andreas did was perfection. Look at the detail on the feathers and the expression of anguish on the...

ARCHIE. Your Honor, there is no need to...

JUDGE. Signor Delancy, you are interrupting?

ARCHIE. Shall I remove my shirt? Shall I bear my back?

JUDGE. Signor, control yourself. I am a married man. Signora continue.

SIGNORA. Andreas spent many days doing what this man wanted. The tattoo of the fall of Icarus on this fiend's back is probably one of Andreas' best works.

JUDGE. I see it in the photographs here. It ranks with the best classical interpretations of Icarus' flight.

ARCHIE. Look, I'm a connoisseur of art. *(She spits on ARCHIE again.)*

JUDGE. Sustained. Go on, my dear lady.

SIGNORA. Andreas worked so long and hard and pushed himself beyond his limits to do the work for this ... this ... this...

ARCHIE. Art connoisseur, that's all. I am an art...

SIGNORA. British plunderer!

ARCHIE. I take offense!

JUDGE. Continue to do so and I'll have you bound and gagged for disrupting an official inquiry. Signora, please, tell all.

SIGNORA. Yes, Your Honor. Andreas was retired. He was a sick man. He was well off once, but our children had squandered all his money. The grandchildren needed clothes. The babies were peeing in our faces for lack of diapers. This rich English pig came waving money and showing Andreas his back. At first, Andreas refused. But this one implored him: "Go ahead, Andreas, you can use the money, and I'll be famous." He even had the tattoo needles and inks with him. Andreas, Your Honor, killed himself staying up late to do *the fall of Icarus*. *(to ARCHIE:)* Murderer!

ARCHIE. I paid 800 lire.

SIGNORA. So what? Andreas is dead. *Dead*.

ARCHIE. Your Honor, I have a receipt from Signora Pincini showing that I paid my bill for services rendered. *(He puts the receipt on the bench.)*

JUDGE. What pervert would want a work of fine art with his body as a background?

ARCHIE. Your Honor, I'm not an artist. The great tragedy in my life is that I am not an artist. I have always been a lover of art, obsessed with the talent of others. Back in England, I am the curator of the fine arts museum in Liverpool. I've always been a custodian of masterpieces. I've always been just a caretaker of great works. I wanted ... I wanted in some way to become a work of art myself. I saw some sailors getting tattooed one day and I hit upon the idea of having one of the great artists of Europe do a work on my flesh.

SIGNORA. You are no better than a whore!

ARCHIE. I was turned down by two French impressionists, a German engraver, and a Viennese realist. But Andreas Pincini...

SIGNORA. Who was famous, but poor...

JUDGE. Living in a remote Italian village...

SIGNORA. You could buy him!

ARCHIE. I commissioned a work of art. My receipt.

JUDGE. Signor Delancy, I don't think you see the whole matter clearly. Why do you think you were detained at our border when you tried to cross into France?

ARCHIE. Because when Andreas died ... *(She spits on ARCHIE'S face.)* When Andreas died, *she* blabbed the whole business to the newspapers. At the border, they made me remove my coat and shirt and show then *the fall of Icarus.* They swooned at the artistry. Then they turned me back. By Italian law, they said, no work of fine art is allowed to leave the country.

JUDGE. And they told you correctly, signor. Two art students in Rome attempted suicide because they thought you got out.

ARCHIE. Really? Two art students? In Rome? Is that so? *(She spits in ARCHIE'S face as before.)* Let me explain further.

JUDGE. There is nothing to explain. You have gotten your wish. You have turned your otherwise worthless back into a work of art. But now you must remain here in Italy.

ARCHIE. That won't be necessary.

JUDGE. Oh, but, it will. Now, you may starve here in our country, or you may earn your keep by sitting bareback in a museum in Torino for six hours daily. Weekends and national holidays excluded.

ARCHIE. But it won't be necessary, You Honor. There's no more problem. You see, as much as I hated to do it, I've got to get home, so I had *the fall of Icarus* covered.

JUDGE. What?!

SIGNORA. Covered?!

ARCHIE. Covered over, yes.

SIGNORA. *You had someone touch Andreas' work?*

ARCHIE. Well, I have to get out of the country. I have to go home. If I'm not allowed to remove Italian art from Italy, surely, I must be allowed to remove Italian art from my back. So you see, there is no more problem. I can go. It hurt me more than it hurt you, and I'm out the 800 lire I paid... *(pause)* Why at you all staring at me? *(The JUDGE signals to POLICEMAN to come forward.)* Look, I have an Aunt Bridie who looks for me to make Christmas ... What's the matter? ... You see, I dress up as old Saint Nick and ... Your Honor?

JUDGE. *What,* Signor, did you do to Andreas Pincini's famous *fall of Icarus?*

ARCHIE. I went to an ordinary tattooist, that's all. For 20 lire he just covered the whole thing over. *(ARCHIE removes his coat and shirt and reveals an English flag tattooed on his back.)* It's the Union Jack, you, know, the British flag... what's the matter? Huh?

SIGNORA. *Signor swine! (She spits in his face again.)*

ARCHIE. *What is it now?*

JUDGE. Signor Delancy, anyone found guilty of defacing a work of fine art in Italy gets up to twenty years in prison!

ARCHIE. What?! *(The POLICEMAN grabs him.)* It was the skin of my back!

JUDGE. When Andreas made his first stroke with the pen, it ceased to be your back. It was his canvas. It was for the ages. It was Pincini's *Fall of Icarus! Now Gone Forever!*

Take him away, officer!

ARCHIE. *(as the OFFICER grabs him)* Wait! Wait!

JUDGE. For what? *The Fall of Icarus* defaced ... destroyed ... after trial, you'll spend twenty years.

ARCHIE. No!

JUDGE. Our works of art must be protected at all cost. *(The crying SIGNORA prepares to spit in ARCHIE'S face again.)*

JUDGE. Signora, please. Enough. He is a fallen man. *(The JUDGE comes down from the bench and approaches ARCHIE. He stops before him.)*

ARCHIE. May I have your final word, Your Honor?

(The JUDGE spits in ARCHIE'S face. The POLICEMAN drags him off. The sobbing SIGNORA PINCINI embraces the JUDGE as the LIGHTS fade.)

DUSK

TIME: Early 20th Century England

PLACE: A London park

AT RISE: A retired gentleman, NORMAN, sits on a park bench, reading a book. Around the bench are fallen leaves and some old newspapers. After a beat, another elderly gentleman, ALLEN, walks by and, with some difficulty, sits at the other end of the bench. NORMAN looks at him until he finally settles on the bench. Then NORMAN returns to his book.

NORMAN. *(reading, almost to himself)* "A king that is conquered must see strange looks, so bitter is the heart of man"...

ALLEN. I beg your pardon. Were you addressing me?

NORMAN. No, no. I'm sorry. I was reading. Sometimes when I'm reading I blurt out some passage that strikes my fancy.

ALLEN. Oh.

NORMAN. Now that I'm retired. I have to sit in the park and read.

ALLEN. Same with me. It's nice. It's nice to have the time to just sit ... just sit and ... and observe humanity.

NORMAN. Yes, it is. And one does become very keen watching them all. The bored housewife. The lad skipping school.

ALLEN. Yes.

NORMAN. The chap out of work. Lovers on lunch break.

ALLEN. You can't miss them.

NORMAN. You get so you can read them.

ALLEN. How's that?

NORMAN. Read them. Their thoughts. Their hopes. Their defects.

ALLEN. Oh, yes. It's true. It makes you a special breed when you retire. You sit and stare like a Buddha. You've seen the world twice, maybe three times over. In fact, more than seen, you've lived it all.

NORMAN. My sentiments exactly. So much wisdom locked in so old a head. A certain conceit sets in, doesn't it?

ALLEN. I know what you mean.

NORMAN. You want to go up to them in a grandfatherly fashion and ... and...

ALLEN. Guide them.

NORMAN. That's it. Guide them. *(He rises.)* Enlighten them. "Don't let that boy speak to you that way; you're his mother," or "School's important for a young chap. Later in life it could pay off well, if you study hard," or "Oh, tell her you love her, sir, life and love go by so damned fast."

ALLEN. Too bad by the time we get to know the world and the people in it, arthritis sets in. These legs. Got to keep stretching them. My name's Allen, sir.

NORMAN. I'm Norman. *(They shake hands.)*

ALLEN. If you'll excuse me now, Norman, I'll stroll a bit more before it gets dark. I'll be back.

NORMAN. *(as ALLEN struggles to his feet)* Yes. Here, let me help you. *(He helps ALLEN up.)* Go on then. Have a pleasant walk. *(He watches ALLEN go off. He picks up his book and sits down again on the bench.)* Nice chap ... Made me lose my place ... Where was I ... Here ...

(As NORMAN reads out loud, a YOUNGER MAN flings himself on to the park bench.)

NORMAN. "A king that is conquered must see strange looks, so bitter a thing is the heart of man..." *(NORMAN looks at the younger man brooding and looking at the ground.)* Your day went poorly.

YOUNG MAN. How could you tell, sir?

NORMAN. Well, I'm a fairly astute observer of our race, and it didn't take much observing to see that you're in poor temper.

YOUNG MAN. You'd be to, if you were in the fix I'm in. I've done the silliest thing.

NORMAN. Oh?

YOUNG MAN. I came up from Dover this afternoon and, oh, forget it. You don't want to hear.

NORMAN. No. No. If it'll help you, spill it out.

YOUNG MAN. *(rising)* I've got to tell someone.

NORMAN. Please, go on.

YOUNG MAN. All right. I came up here to London from Dover this afternoon on business for my firm and took a place in a small family-run hotel. It was a nice room, but there was no soap, so I went out to buy a cake. After I bought the soap I ... I don't know ... I started to walk the streets. London is a Mecca for the casual stroller, the brouser, you know.

NORMAN. That's true. It is.

YOUNG MAN. Then I had a drink at the quaintest little pub. After that I walked some more. Suddenly, I realized — and this sounds remarkably stupid — I realized I couldn't remember the name of the small hotel or the street where I was staying.

NORMAN. Oh, no.

YOUNG MAN. Yes. I tried to back track and found myself in still another area I didn't recognize. I took still another direction and wound up in this park here. How's that for a dilemma? And me who hasn't got a friend or connection in London.

NORMAN. I could give you the name of a small place where you could be comfortable until you can...

YOUNG MAN. And pay for it with what? I came out with only some change which I spent on the soap and the drink. My wallet's back wherever it is I was staying.

NORMAN. That is a dilemma, young man.

YOUNG MAN. It's Friday night, so I can't wire my firm for funds until Monday mornng at 8:30. So here I am in the park with no money and no where to go. *(Pause. The YOUNG MAN sits back down.)*

NORMAN. Quite a problem. Quite a story.

YOUNG MAN. I suppose — I mean, I take from your tone — that you think I've spun an impossible yarn.

NORMAN. Impossible? No. Anyone can lose his way in a strange city. It happened years ago to me. In Rome.

YOUNG MAN. Then you understand how chilling it is to be out in the cold.

NORMAN. Yes, of course, I understand.

YOUNG MAN. Unless ... unless I can find some decent, understanding good Samaritan to see me for what I am, a victim of circumstances, and lend me some money, I'm ... I'm likely to spend the night here sleeping on this bench. *(Pause. He looks at NORMAN.)*

NORMAN. Yes, well, that is the case as you've spelled it out. But there are plenty of decent people in the world, my young friend, who would lend you the money for your lodging.

YOUNG MAN. Do you really think so, sir?

NORMAN. Yes, I do. That is if you could...

YOUNG MAN. Could what? Could what, sir?

NORMAN. If you could ... produce the soap.

YOUNG MAN. If I ... If I ... I could...

NORMAN. That's right. *(The YOUNG MAN gets up and looks through his pockets.)*

YOUNG MAN. The ... the soap ... I ... God in heaven, I must've lost it.

NORMAN. To lose a small hotel and a cake of soap in one afternoon is bad luck.

YOUNG MAN. But I ... I ... all right ... Never mind, sir. Never mind. *(The YOUNG MAN walks away dejected. NORMAN rises and looks afters him. Then he begins to laugh.)*

NORMAN. Pity. The going out to get the soap was the one convincing touch in the whole fabrication. If he had thought to actually buy a bar, he probably could've convinced me to ... to ... *(He sees something behind the bench. He bends over and picks it up. It is a cake of soap.)* Soap! Evidently, it fell from his pocket. Evidently, the young man was ... *(NORMAN crosses and calls off stage.)* You there! Young man! Hello there, young man! I say, come back! Please!

Do come back!

(The YOUNG MAN re-enters.)

YOUNG MAN. What is it then? *(NORMAN holds up the bar of soap. The YOUNG MAN looks at it.)*

NORMAN. It must've slid out of your overcoat when you sat down. I saw it on the ground after you left. You'll have to excuse my disbelief. But appearances were really against you. I'm a rather good judge, normally, of people. *(He hands the YOUNG MAN the soap.)* Here. And accept my apologies.

YOUNG MAN. Lucky thing... you finding it. *(NORMAN takes out his wallet.)*

NORMAN. Yes. Take this money and this card with my address. Any day next week will do for returning the money. *(The YOUNG MAN takes the money and the card.)*

YOUNG MAN. Thank you, sir. You are my savior this day.

NORMAN. Don't mention it.

YOUNG MAN. You're too modest. How many people would give a stranger money?

NORMAN. But I am a good judge of people, and now I know you'll return it.

YOUNG MAN. Oh, I will, sir. Monday morning, sir. I'd better go get myself settled. Until next week then. Goodbye, sir. *(He shakes NORMAN'S hand and Exits, pleased.)*

NORMAN. *(calling off)* And don't lose your soap again. It's been a good friend to you ... Poor boy. *(NORMAN crosses back to the bench and sits.)* Heavens, the light's almost gone. Dusk. I should finish this chapter. *(He opens the book.)* Where is it now that I left... Yes, here... "A king that is conquered must see strange looks, so bitter a thing is the heart of man...

(ALLEN re-enters. NORMAN continues reading silently. ALLEN crosses to the bench and begins to poke around in the leaves and newspapers.)

NORMAN. Have a nice stroll, did you, Allen?
ALLEN. Yes. Yes I did, Norman.
NORMAN. Have you lost something?
ALLEN. Yes, Norman, a cake of soap...

(ALLEN continues poking around as NORMAN puts his book down snd stares straight ahead and the LIGHTS fade.)

Other Publications for Your Interest

PASTORAL
(COMEDY)
By PETER MALONEY

1 man, 1 woman—Exterior

Daniel Stern ("Blue Thunder", "Breaking Away") and Kristin Griffith ("The Europeans", "Interiors") starred originally at NYC's famed Ensemble Studio Theatre in the preceptive comedy about a city couple temporarily tending a farm. He hates the bucolic life and is terrified, for instance, by such horrors as a crowing rooster; whereas she is at one with the land *and* the rooster. "An endearing picture of young love at a comic crossroads."—N.Y. Times. "Sharp, satiric humor."—New Yorker. "An audience pleaser."—Village Voice. Published with *Last Chance Texaco*. (#17995)

LAST CHANCE TEXACO
(DRAMA)
By PETER MALONEY

3 women—Interior

Originally staged to great acclaim at NYC's famed Ensemble Studio Theatre, this is a haunting, lyrical play set in the American Garage, a Texaco station in a small Texas town run by a mother and her daughter. Late one night, while driving through, a city woman named Ruth has a flat tire, an occurrence which causes her own unusual life to intersect with Verna and Cissy, as they fix her tire in the American Garage. This play is an excellent source of monologue and scene material. It is also a gripping piece of theatre. Published with *Pastoral*. (#13887)

BUSINESSMAN'S LUNCH
(COMEDY)
By MICHAEL QUINN

4 men, 1 woman—Interior

Originally produced by the famed Actors Theatre of Louisville, this marked the debut of a wonderful new comic playwriting voice. We are in one of those quiche-and-salad restaurants, where three high-powered young executives of a nearby candy company are having lunch as they discuss company politics and various marketing and advertising strategies. They particularly enjoy making fun of one of their fellows who is not present, whom they consider a hopeless nerd—until, that is, they learn that he is engaged to marry the boss's daughter. "Cleverly skewers corporate stereotypes."—NY Times. (#4712)

Other Publications for Your Interest

THE SQUARE ROOT OF LOVE
(ALL GROUPS—FOUR COMEDIES)

By DANIEL MELTZER

1 man, 1 woman—4 Simple Interiors

This full-length evening portrays four preludes to love—from youth to old age, from innocence to maturity. Best when played by a single actor and actress. **The Square Root of Love.** Two genius-level college students discover that Man (or Woman) does not live by intellectual pursuits alone . . . **A Good Time for a Change.** Our couple are now a successful executive and her handsome young male secretary. He has decided it's time for a change, and so has she . . . **The Battling Brinkmires.** George and Marsha Brinkmire, a middle-aged couple, have come to Haiti to get a "quickie" divorce. This one has a surprise ending . . . **Waiting For To Go.** We are on a jet waiting to take off for Florida. He's a retired plumbing contractor who thinks his life is over—she's a recent widow returning to her home in Hallandale. The play, and the evening, ends with a beginning . . . A success at off-off Broadway's Hunter Playwrights. Requires only minimal settings. (#21314)

SNOW LEOPARDS
(LITTLE THEATRE—COMIC DRAMA)

By MARTIN JONES

2 women—Exterior

This haunting little gem of a play was a recent crowd-pleaser Off Off Broadway in New York City, produced by the fine StageArts Theatre Co. Set in Lincoln Park Zoo in Chicago in front of the snow leopards' pen, the play tells the story of two sisters from rural West Virginia. When we first meet Sally, she has run away from home to find her big sister Claire June, whose life Up North she has imagined to be filled with all the promise and hopes so lacking Down Home. Turns out, life in the Big City ain't all Sally and C.J. thought it would be; but Sally is going to stay anyway, and try to make her way. "Affecting and carefully crafted . . . a moving piece of work."—New York City Tribune. *Actresses take note*: this play is a treasure trove of scene and monologue material. *Producers take note*: the play may be staged simply and inexpensively. (#21245)

Other Publications for Your Interest

ADVICE TO THE PLAYERS
(DRAMA)

By BRUCE BONAFEDE

5 men, 1 woman (interracial)—Interior

Seldom has a one-act play created such a sensation as did *Advice to the Players* at Actors Theatre of Louisville's famed Humana Festival of New American Plays. Mr. Bonafede has crafted an ingenious play about two Black South African actors, here in America to perform their internationally-acclaimed production of *Waiting for Godot*. The victims of persecution in their own country, here in the U.S. they become the victims of a different kind of persecution. The anti-apartheid movement wants a strong political gesture—they want the performance cancelled. And, they are willing to go to any lengths to achieve this aim— including threatening the families of the actors back home. Cleverly, Mr. Bonafede juxtaposes the predicament of Didi and Gogo in *Waiting for Godot* with the predicament of the two actors. Both, in an odd, ironic way, are Theatre of the Absurd. "A short play blazing with emotional force and moral complexities . . . taut, searing inquiry into the inequities frequently perpetrated in the name of political justice . . . a stunning moment of theatrical truth."—Louisville Courier-Journal. (#3027)

APPROACHING LAVENDAR
(COMIC DRAMA)

By JULIE BECKETT CRUTCHER

3 women—Interior

While their father is marrying his fourth wife sardonic, controlled Jenny and her slightly neurotic housewife-sister Abigail wait in a church vestibule. There they encounter Wren, the spacey ingenue who is about to become their step-sister. The mood of polite tolerance degenerates with comic results as inherent tensions mount and the womens' conflicted feelings about their parents' remarriage surface. The contingent self-discovery results in new understanding and forgiveness, and ultimately reveals the significance of sisterhood. Highly-praised in its debut at the famed Actors Theatre of Louisville, the play was singled out by the Louisville press for its "precise and disquieting vision" as well as its sharp humor, as it "held a capacity audience rapt." (#3649)

A TANTALIZING
(DRAMA)

By WILLIAM MASTROSIMONE

1 man, 1 woman—Interior

Originally produced by the amazing Actors Theatre of Louisville, this is a new one-act drama by the author of *The Woolgatherer* and *Extremities*. *A Tantalizing* is about the attempts by a young woman to "save" a street bum, a tattered and crazy old man whom she has dragged in off the street. Like Rose in *Extremities* she, too, has secrets in her closet. What these secrets are is the intriguing mystery in the plot of the play, as we gradually realize why the woman has taken such an interest in the bum. (#22021)

Other Publications for Your Interest

VIVIEN
(COMIC DRAMA)
By PERCY GRANGER

2 men, 1 woman—Unit set

Recently staged to acclaim at Lincoln Center, this lovely piece is about a young stage director who visits his long-lost father in a nursing home and takes him to see a production of "The Seagull" that he staged. Along the way, each reveals a substantial truth about himself, and the journey eventually reaches its zenith in a restaurant after the performance. "A revealing father-son portrait that gives additional certification to the author's position as a very original playwright."—N.Y. Times. "The dialogue has the accuracy of real people talking."—N.Y. Post.

LANDSCAPE WITH WAITRESS
(COMEDY)
By ROBERT PINE

1 man, 1 woman—Interior

Arthur Granger is an unsuccessful novelist who lives a Walter Mitty-like fantasy existence. Tonight, he is dining out in an Italian restaurant which seems to have only one waitress and one customer—himself. As Arthur selects his dinner he has fantasies of romantic conquest, which he confides to the audience and to his notebook. While Arthur's fantasies take him into far-fetched plots, the waitress acts out the various characters in his fantasy. Soon, Arthur is chattering and dreaming away at such a quick clip that neither he nor we can be entirely sure of his sanity. Arthur finishes his dinner and goes home, ending as he began—as a lover *manqué*. " . . . a landscape of the mind."—Other Stages. " . . . has moments of true originality and a bizarre sense of humor . . . a devious and slightly demented half-hour of comedy."—N.Y. Times. Recently a hit at New York's excellent Ensemble Studio Theatre.

Other Publications for Your Interest

MOVIE OF THE MONTH
(COMEDY)
By DANIEL MELTZER

2 men—Interior

This new comedy by the author of the ever-popular *The Square Root of Love* is an amusing satire of commercial television. B.S., a TV programming executive, is anxious to bolster his network's ratings, which have been sagging of late due to programming disasters such as a documentary called "The Ugly Truth" (says B.S.: "What the hell is The Ugly Truth, and how the hell did it get into our Prime Time?") His eagerbeaver assistant, appropriately named Broun, has found a script which he is sure can be made into a hit "Movie of the Month". It's about this Danish prince, see, who comes home from college to find that his uncle has murdered his father and married his mother . . . Well, naturally, B.S. has his own ideas about how to fix such a totally unbelievable plot . . . (#17621)

SUNDANCE
(ALL GROUPS—COMEDY)
By MEIR Z. RIBALOW

5 men—Simple interior

This new comedy from the author of *Shrunken Heads* is set in a sort of metaphysical wild west saloon. The characters include Hickock, Jesse, the Kid, and the inevitable Barkeep. Hickock kills to uphold the law. Jesse kills for pleasure. The Kid kills to bring down The Establishment. What if, wonders the Barkeep, they met up with the Ultimate Killer—who kills for no reason, who kills simply because that's what he does? Enter Sundance. He does not kill to uphold the law, for pleasure, or to make a political statement, or because he had a deprived childhood. And he proceeds to kill everyone, exiting at the end with his sixguns blazing! "Witty, strong, precise, unusually well-written."—The Guardian. "A brilliant piece."—Dublin Evening Press. This co-winner of the 1981 Annual NYC Metropolitan Short Play Festival has been a success in 6 countries! (#3113)